Cloud of Dauphin Island

written by

Sandra Mafera

Illustrations by Sarah Koldewey

AuthorHouse™
1663 Liberty Drive, Suite 200
Bloomington, IN 47403
www.authorhouse.com
Phone: 1-800-839-8640

© 2009 Sandra Mafera. All rights reserved.
No part of this book may be reproduced, stored in a retrieval system, or transmitted by any means without the written permission of the author.

First published by AuthorHouse 2/24/2009

ISBN: 978-1-4389-5159-1 (sc)

Printed in the United States of America
Bloomington, Indiana

This book is printed on acid-free paper.
Illustrations 2008 by Sarah Koldewey

The illustration artwork is done in ink and watercolor.

To: My Granddaughters
Jessica, Natalie, Anna and Emilia
Blessing me with joy,
G-Ma

"Shoo, shoo," says G-ma as a white bird lands on the railing of the deck. "Go on now, shoo." G-ma waves her hand in a sweeping motion. Instead, the bird struts back and forth as if to say, "Could we be friends?"

She is a beauty. She is pure white with a red-pink beak that matches her feet. There is a small tuft on the back of her head and her wings form a perfect V with her tail feathers. She parades, lifting her feet as if she is marching. She shows her best steps with her head held high.

"Anna, come see this bird. Isn't she beautiful?"

"Where did she come from?" asks Anna

The bird hops to the back of a deck chair. "Whoa, come on little birdie; that's too close now. Shoo!"

She hops back on the railing and continues to strut back and forth, forth and back. While she cranes her neck and preens her bright white feathers, her brilliant black eyes watch them every moment.

Anna is delighted.

"Well, aren't you the brave one!" says G-ma. The bird flutters to the table, closer and closer. She makes a soft sound as if she wants to talk.

"Well, Anna, if she wants to be friends, what would you like to name her?"

"Hmm, I think Cloud would be a good name."
"Don't you think she is pretty brazen for such a nice name?" asks G-ma.

"She is so white and fluffy, I think Cloud is a perfect name," declares Anna.

"So be it; Cloud is what we will call her."

And like a cloud she floats off toward the bay. The bright sun glances off her wings as Cloud gets smaller and smaller.

"Well, that was fun. What a nice visit from a stranger while we vacation on Dauphin Island," says G-ma.

They are off to the Lighthouse Bakery for scrumptious turnovers, croissants and cinnamon rolls.

They visit Fort Gaines at the end of Dauphin Island and then go back to the bakery for sandwiches, soup and fresh baked cookies before returning to the cottage.

"Anna, look who is back for a visit!"

Anna calls, "Cloud!" and the bird turns her head as if she knows her name. Cloud hops from the railing to the back of the chair again. This time they don't say, "shoo," but watch, enchanted that she has come for another visit.

She floats from the chair to the tabletop, so close Anna and G-ma can touch her. But they don't. Her brilliant white feathers look like they were cast perfectly by her creator. They listen as she makes the soft sounds and walks slowly back and forth right in front of them.

Anna frets, "She must be someone's pet because she is not afraid. Do you think she got carried along by the winds of the hurricane and can't find her way home?"

"Maybe she is hungry."

In the pantry they find a bag of birdseed. Anna wonders if perhaps Cloud comes often and other visitors have fed her.

The evening turns chilly, Cloud returns to the deck and perches on the back of a chair. She fluffs her feathers, and her head almost disappears between her wings.

She just roosts and rests within touching distance. She is now a welcome guest. Anna and G-ma spread some seed along the railing and she hops up to tap, tap, tap as she chooses her favorite seeds.

When the sun comes up, Cloud is resting on the front deck. Anna and G-ma say good morning, and she prances along the railing in a royal show of friendship. Then she is off on another journey. She doesn't seem to have friends, as do the big gray pigeons that swoop below the deck to eat the seeds that fall from the railing. Even the monarch butterflies are in groups as they flutter near the bushes.

No, Cloud is alone.

Anna and G-ma are off on a journey too.

They want to explore the island and swim in the ocean.

When they return, Cloud is there waiting. She coos a while and Anna gets the birdseed. Cloud moves ever closer and closer to G-ma. It is as if she wants to share a secret. She walks along the railing until she is in front of G-ma.

Then Cloud does a most unusual thing. She hops from the railing to G-ma's shoulder!

G-ma is not at all afraid.

Cloud perches close to G-ma's ear as if to share a secret.

G-ma listens, but Cloud hops again—

—this time to the top of G-ma's head!

Anna and G-ma giggle, laugh and wonder at this funny bird. She certainly is not afraid of them. "She must trust us a lot," says Anna.

Cloud knows they like her too.

It is sad to leave Dauphin Island.

G-ma says, "I think Cloud wants us to remember her and come back to Dauphin Island again soon."

On the long ride home, Anna asks, "What did Cloud whisper in your ear, G-ma?"

G-ma smiles. "She told me . . .

'Remember to be brave even when you're not.
Be the best you can be.'"

Lightning Source UK Ltd.
Milton Keynes UK
UKRC01n0800190917
309433UK00009B/34